Social Injustice

Path to Nihilism:

Perspectives in Black and Beyond

By:

Brian Swanson

All rights reserved.

No part of this book my be reproduced, stored in a retrieval system or transmitted in any form or by any means without the prior written permission of the author and/or publisher except by a reviewer who may quote brief passages for print in a newspaper, magazine or journal, and online retail platforms.

Second Edition

Copyright 1997, 2021

At the specific preference of the author, this work remains as the author intended, verbatim, and with minimal editorial input.

ISBN: 978-1-950438-15-0

Cover art by:

Kenny Highborn

Published by:

MAJart Works

2001 NE Aloclek Dr Suite 211

Hillsboro, OR 97124

www.majartworks.com

Inside Lines:

In Retrospect
Classism
Genocide
Hatred
War
Reflection

Summary /Purpose

Nihilism- A total rejection of all existing principles, values and institutions.

This book of Social-Political prose focuses on the effects of Classism, Genocide, Hatred and War.

How they effect Black People and other minorities.

Shedding light on how these four factors affect other minorities roles in society and how they are treated.

Most importantly, it shows how disoriented society becomes when it tries to close itself off. How people handle the responsibility of being human.

Written in 1997 these things are still very poignant and relevant work and should be read with an open Mind.

In Retrospect

African Warrior

The African warrior planted its foot in the sand.
Leaving a distinct imprint on the form and
civilization of man.
The warrior taken from its homeland,
on board a ship of oppression bound for a new land.

The warrior in chains, but its spirit is still free.
Leaving a footprint in the sand,
making it possible for us to stand.

The warrior spirit has taken the form of Harriet Tubman who left her
indelible footprints while guiding her people through the dark southern
wilderness,
to that beacon of northern light called freedom.

The warrior has taken the form of Frederick Douglas, who helped to
make strides in the abolishment of slavery, and who left a big imprint
of thought in the sands of American history.

The warrior has also taken the forms of George Washington Carver,
Benjamin Banneker, Dr. Charles Drew, and Garret A. Morgan.
Showing the ingenuity and fortitude of invention, leaving a distinct imprint in the everyday lives of American society.

The warrior spirit also took the form of Ida B. Wells who wrote about
the lynching's of black-Americans and brought to light the injustices of
hatred toward the most persecuted beings.
The warrior has been Carter G. Woodson, Booker Washington, Marcus
Garvey, and W.E.B. Dubois. All left giant footprints in the form of intel-

lectual conversation and stimulation of thought about the role of Black people in American Society.

The warrior's spirit also shone through in voice, with the likes of Mahalia Jackson and Marian Anderson singing to soothe the savage beasts of the day.
Then in 1936, the warrior stood in the form of Jesse Owens. Dashing Hitler's myth of the Master Race and leaving big footsteps in the myth and ideology of racial superiority.

In WW II, the warrior's fighting spirit took shape in the Tuskegee Airmen, who proved that Black people were-
Smart enough!
Dedicated enough! And
Brave enough!
To fight for and defend this country, even though they were treated as second class citizens.

And 50 years ago, the warrior stood in the form of Jackie Robinson at Ebbets Field. Bearing the brunt of taunts and epithets, and yet he still stood on first base, sacrificed himself for second base, took third, and stole home! Breaking the barriers in America's
two favorite past-times-
Baseball and racism!

Then in 1955 the African Warrior took the form of Rosa Parks, who refused to move to the back of the bus. And by not moving she lit the fire of a movement for
Civil Rights.

Then the Warrior became Martin Luther King, marching for freedom and uttering his dream in the air of hostility, hoping to provide a foundation of hope on which to stand and be counted.

The warrior is also Malcom X standing and delivering his message of Black empowerment, and self-improvement.   Wanting to lead his people from the ruins of self-hatred to the stark reality of self-love.

The warrior also showed himself in the spirits of Bob Marley and Stevie Wonder. Having the courage to deliver messages of love in the air of persecution. And stirring the consciousness of people through the genius of their music.
Even though the warrior has taken on a more modern form, it still faces a lot of old problems.

The warrior continues the fight!
The warrior continues the struggle!
To reach the boundless landscape of freedom.
Now the warrior looks at a shadow of its future self, and it urges the shadow to continue the journey toward freedom in this nation. Not just for modern prosperity but those lost sands of African Civilizations.

Classism

Act of showing prejudice or extreme dislike toward an individual because of their social rank, status, or level.

Black Dust
Street
Wrong
The Migrant Workers Song
The Wall
People on the Wall

Black Dust

Timeless Black Dust Rises from the dusk of the sand.
Black Dust is rising where the clouds sit in smoke.
Black dust is riding into the consciousness of the land.
Black Dust is bearing the torment of the earth.

 -But

Where the dust rises it will soon fall.
Where the dust is rising it will soon drop.
where the dust is bearing, there it will live.
But wherever there is dust there is man.

Wrong

Everybody says I live on the wrong side of town
But who says my side's wrong.
If you look at the map that is when you see,
there is no right or wrong side to believe.
Everybody says I live on the wrong side of town,
But everybody does not know me.

They put me in with the statistics and stereotypes, because-
they think everybody from my part of town is alike.
Since I do not count as a human or as an individual,
just another pronoun or a bad apple.
Everybody says I live on the wrong side of town
But everybody really does not know me.

All of them see with blinders on,
drawing distinct invisible boundaries.
You all know them as:
across the river,
by the bridge,
through the meadow, or
on oak ridge.
It is behind the store
near the suburbs, and
across the railroad tracks.
And everybody says I live on the wrong side of town
but everybody really does not know me.

For I have been stereotyped and generalized,
while my part of town is paralyzed.
All you see is a decrepit building and a broken window,
but there is a broken promise and a crooked swindle.

Everybody says I live on the wrong side of town ,while
all these bullshit ideologies come flaming aground.
I'm not counted! and I'm not seen !
So how does anybody know if I'm tough or mean.
On those physical invisible boundaries a wall is built,
to separate those in high places from their guilt,

Yes! I'm impoverished and that is a fact
for I live on the wall beneath its' cracks.

Everybody says I live on the wrong side of town

But everybody does not know me.

Street

Yo! I'm here to tell you about a place I know.
It runs and festers, and it stinks.
It is my Mom, my Dad, and my whole family.
You may call it run down, but I call it the street.
This is not the street that is paved with gold
but to live on it you must be bold.
For out here you do not decide your fate or your destiny.
Because the only thing that matters is survival!
Survival is the name of the game, if you do not
learn quick you just end up dead.
Yo! To you I may be an aimless wanderer looking for
a place to go
whose
destination is unknown. A tired and weary man
who has nothing left on which to stand. I could be that
bum who sleeps on cold pavement, or I could be that
homeboy who lives in the ghetto. For we are all one
person, one race, one nation, and it is called the **Street!**

We are the underclass or of the no class,
we are the bottom rung of the ladder! And-
live on the low end of the totem pole! But one
thing you do is close your eyes and wish it will go away,
but you fail to realize that we are here to stay.

We are locked in on those streets of mean
while everybody else chases the American dream.
While you go off and join the rat race
I live with the rats trying to save face.

If you do not believe this world exists
then I know you are full of shit!
The government promises false hope and a dream,
and all they see is shattered glass and a broken pipe.
I see a shattered dream and a broken promise.
As the distant wind blows all that away
the promises of a better tomorrow do not even hold sway.

Everybody from Jessie Jackson to the President is saying
"we are trying to do our best, just keep hope alive".
But I think they are all full of crap,
for they fail to look and see where I'm at.
I'm the underbelly of society, who languishes
in the dark corner of it, never-
to be found, located, heard, or felt!

And no one cares.

Out here on the street, you only get respect if-
you either have the most grip, or the best gat. You have
lots of money or you have a tech- nine with a banana clip.

Out here on the street:
Frustration is my big brother!
Despair is my little sister! And-
Rage is my cousin!

They are all related to me and to the street.
They are the only family I have to fall back on,
the only ones that seem to care.

While you wake up to a nice warm bed
I wake up to peeling off yesterday's newspaper instead.
You may wake up to a hot breakfast, I wake up to a
black dude smiling on the cream of wheat box,
and I wonder what the hell he's got to be so damn happy about. I have
to go out and face that cold hard concrete
of shattered dreams and broken promises.

Where-
poverty runs rampant,
disease is a panther on the prowl,
kids having kids, and throwing them away
trying to protect them from having live this way.

Where-

drugs kill and shatters future and present hopes. And-
the suffocating reality of it all, is that it seems it will
cave in on us, the underclass! And there seems to be no way out.
As the sunsets, and casts a grim and bleak shadow on that cold hard street.
The life you live out here is filled with bitterness at every defeat.

This you may call a rat infested, drug infested , hell-hole
but I call it home, the place where the roaches roam.
The reward for being out here is hard, it either
sharing a small cell with big Buck or lonely Billy Joe
while death's destiny comes knocking on your door.
The other reward is being buried six feet under
those shattered dreams and broken promises.

As the sirens roar, and the gunfire hails
the night is of an eerie still. And
as the street lamps grow dim,
it casts a reflection of an underclass of people,

A people of lost hope.
This reflection sheds new light on that-
quiet, pulsating, stalking animal
of a different breed called-

The Street.

The Migrant Worker's Song

My flesh is melting under the glare
of persecution from the sun.
My hands are sweaty, and are
starting to cramp-up and crumble because,
of the constant picking of
fruits and vegetables that do not show-up on my table.

If you looked at my skin,
you will see the deep welts of torment
embedded in the flesh of hope.
You will see the scars from the tears and blood
that lead to a path of injustices.
The sweat that pours off my back shows-up in the form
of green backs which I always lack.

And-

I - the laborer live on the land,
work on the land, and
own no parts of it!

I - the laborer live with the
sun as my overseer, and
time as my torment.

I - the laborer pick-up and
move when the seasons change,
in order to pick-up more work.

I - the laborer incur the wrath
of grapes in the vineyards of despair.

How can grapes sell for $.69 a pound
in the grocery store and sell anywhere from
$5- $1000 dollars in a bottle of wine?

It is because-
I - the laborer spend endless days
blistering my hands, and
breaking my back, like a
beast of burden in the field.
I - the laborer sweat and toil
and bleed for a shade of hope
under the sun's oppression,
in the landscape of the
American Nightmare which enslaves me.

But-

As the wind blows the dust of
reality in my face.
My calluses are my honor,
My scars are my story,
My sweat and blood
is the uncircumcised hope
for a better way of living.
My back ache is for the land,
which I own no parts of.
My feet is for the migration
of my service, and the
uncertainty of my existence. It is to

Which ever way the wind blows,
and to which ever land holds the
most promise of a brighter tomorrow.
My flesh still melts under the persecution
from the sun, which is casting
a grim shadow on my existence.
Now I realize that the only thing
I live for are My seeds! My offspring!
And now I plant them on the
realm of the American Nightmare.
In the soil of dreams, so
they can use the overseers persecution
and nature's tears
to sprout forth from the
American Nightmare and
reach **The American Dream.**

The Wall

Look! Down at the hard concrete
Rise! And face a wall at attention
for all the world to see.
It is not just a wall made of brick or stone,
but of tragedies and heartbreak.
If the wall could tell a story,
it would take a thousand millenniums.
If the wall could feel any emotion,
it would heal the broken hearts of the lonely,
and the damaged hopes of the few.

For now at least, the wall says nothing
or feels nothing; but it reflects the pain
and the losses of a new war.
A new search for survival
in the concrete jungle of mankind.
The wall serves as a buffer between the
generations of the dazed and confused and
the generations of the hopeful.

And-

From time to time the wall reflects
a striking image of itself on cold hard concrete
called the streets.
The streets breathe a different breath-
rough and rugged, soft yet subtle.

They cry in outrage over the travesties of injustice. They boil and erupt in anger at the petulant rays of the sun. And underneath the streets voices are heard gnashing and gnawing against the wall of chaos. In the context of all things considered the streets are strange and unique; wholesome yet hostile. And from underneath the streets the voices are heard again, bouncing off the walls of chaos and seeping into the cracks of this present time.

People on the wall

People on the wall but never standing
living lives denied. In spirit they
creep and crawl over gray colored
tombstones and ash-colored roses.
They have become part of statistics,
numbers, and percentages;   yet-
they live on in the memories of
yesterday and the forgotten dreams
of tomorrow.

People on the wall but never standing-
who never got a chance to write their
full histories or legacies.
They lived but were dying.
They saw yet they were blind.
They heard yet they were deaf.
Now reality has locked them up
in a bottomless pit of no beginnings
and no endings. A cruel heartless
place where they sleep and slumber in
times of warning.

People on the wall but never standing,
who always yearned for acceptance,
or a place to fit in; in the complex
jigsaw puzzle that is the street.
They yearned for freedom, yet
they were slaves to a jungle
that promised them everything

and delivered nothing but memories
gone but not forgotten.

People on the wall but never standing
going by aliases of: Mookie, Skeeter,
Lucky, Black, Pitch, Dat Nigga, Toast,
Frog, Roach, Pickle, Sunny, Doothy,
Fat ass, Pepsi, Lil' Slim, and etc...

These are people who lived too
fast, died too young, or were
in the wrong place at the wrong
day and time.

They all had something in common though.
They were searching to find themselves in
a vast ocean of chaos.
They were searching to find peace in
a volatile world of cruelty. They finally
found their peace in this existence, but
the sad thing is they had to pay the
ultimate price- **life.**

But the world still goes on,
not knowing, caring, or
feeling for inhabitants left behind.
These are people on the wall,
who never got a chance to stand!

Genocide

The deliberate and systematic destruction of a racial, political, or cultural group.

Searching

Homicide (A Short Story)

Kill the Indian! Save the Man!

G. B. N

Young, Black, & Handcuffed

De La Coeur

Searching

Crawling in the crawl-space of time looking for a way out.
Searching for the dusk of ideas in the ashbin of life.
But the only reality we face is that of a gun or a knife.
And damned be our pride by the inner workings of self doubt.

Languishing in the corner looking for employment.
While we have become the subject of increasing statistics.
To be locked in jail facing a harsh existence.
Yet and still some of us are still waiting for the government.

To be rendered powerless by splif, dujie, white lady, and angel dust.
Hanging on Lennox and 125th street smoking weed.
Trying to solve the cities problems, and trying to fill a need.
And all these things seem nothing but a puff.

Ignorance sets in and we do not seem to understand,
That society has willed all these evils to be so.
And our second class education has got to go.
And this is why we are children searching in the promised land.

This is a narrative poem based on the book Manchild in the Promised Land.
Written by Claude Brown

Homicide: A Short-Story about Black on Black crime

Another headline! Another damn statistic!
A young brother lies bleeding on the cold pavement of obscurity. After having a useless argument over some Jordan's, I got shot. I lie here bleeding because I would not give up my $110 Jordan's I had worked so long and hard to get. I can not believe Clarence did it, dat nigga shot me! Dat nigga shot me!

As I lay here bleeding unmercifully on this cold pavement of reality; I hear the ambulance coming, the sirens wailing in the background of darkest night, and the stretcher being brought forth to carry my lifeless body.
In the distance there is a chalk outline of my body drawn on the street. The cops are trying to find the weapon, and are milling around collecting evidence and blood. Meanwhile, the paramedics are trying to revive me. They are trying to wake me up from a nightmarish world of hell and fury.
Nevertheless, the EKG machine is working overtime to bring me back, but I'm bleeding profusely. Then there is the pall of silence as the machine keeps going, beep! Beep! Beep! Beep! I finally feel my life slipping from my grasp. I start thinking about those plans for college that will just fade, and never materialize.

Because on this awe struck evening I was shot, by a young brother about my age.

As I'm dying I can still see his face, and the look of uncertainty on him. I could see him wondering why he did it, and for what reasons? Did he really need my shoes?

Was this a gang-related assault, or what?
I will never know any of these answers.
As I'm remembering his face the paramedics are now trying to shock the life back into me, but this is failing miserably. The machine now goes from, Beep! Beep! To that infamous whine of death, which is D-ning- ning-ning-ning-ning-ning-nming-ning- ning-ning-ning-ning-ning-ning-ning.

That is it, my life is over and done with. My life taken out in typical street fashion, sad isn't it!
This is not just one life lost but two. I died not knowing the inside of a college or of the workplace; and the only inside he will see is the one that says State Penn.

For this may seem wild and **black** to you, but it is the truth. For when you loose two young black lives in the process of taking one, it makes for a sad and bleak black existence. With everyone hoping to avoid becoming one of those Black headlines! And Black Statistics!

Think about it.

Kill the Indian! Save the man!

Kill the Indian! Save the Man!
We- The founders of a great nation
long before it achieved its' independence.
We- The natives, the ones with restless
tongues and nomadic feet -
Still suffering from the self-inflicted
wounds of hatred; and
from the brutal conception
of greed in the name of progress!
And it is I - Sitting Bull, Geronimo, and Crazy Horse,
the Indian hiding in the background of society,
now being cut-out of its woven fabric.

Kill the Indian! Save the Man!
From the dawn of manifest destiny,
to the dusk of frontier development.
The lies told- and
The promises made then broken- and
The people hired-
To keep the natives down, and
destroy their spirit with the free
reign of oppression, in the name
of morality!

Kill the Indian! Save the Man!
Fighting for the native land,
which holds generations of
bloodshed underground.

Fighting for the land that
was lusted after by everyone
moving toward the space where
the sun sets.
The land- Our sacred sacrament
Our belief,
Our life, power, strength, and faith.
Taken away by negotiations, and
a hail of bullets and gun-smoke.

The Indian Killed! The Man Saved!
The trail of destruction blazed.
Home we left! Our land we left!
Although we still live on it,
we have to make **reservations**!
We have to make **reservations**!
And that is where the river called
the Trail of Tears runs.

G.B.N   Guns, Blood, & A Nigga

Guns

Guns are the manifestation of violence.
The mere tearing down of peace by the
bulldozer of chaos. Guns represent
the despair and the desperation;-
which provide quick solutions
in this a war bound generation.
They represent the impatience
of communication, which provide
a viable alternative in tight situations.
They represent the need for security,
The need for protection, and serve as
a shield from the rest of the harm-seekers
of the world. Guns are handled, loaded, and
then the trigger is pulled. A cold bullet pierces
the air of reality of the time. It hits a target
standing, walking, and breathing. Then there is
Blood.

Blood

The blood represents life.
It flows from all angles, and
all corners in this vestige of humanity.
The blood has no sound.
The blood is yearning to free
itself to the deity above.
The blood is running toward
an uncertain time, trying to

cross the generation gap.
Trying to fill the time, until
it slowly passes from this earth.
The blood,
the beginning,
the life,
the origin.
Is now spewing out immensely, and
soon shall meet its' resting place in
a sewer drain of turmoil.

Then there is a Nigga lying still.
A tear is shed as his life is passing.
The tear is for the remembrance
of the things past and present,
and for the future that is lost.
The tear streams down the cheek,
trying to find the blood. The
blood is trying to find the black-man.
But where the fuck is he?
Where is the Black-Man?
Where the hell is the Black-Man?
The blood asked the tear, -
The tear had no answer.
The blood kept looking, kept
searching, kept asking, but to no avail.
Until the tear said, from the
shadow of the eye, "I have
found him".
The blood asked "where?"
The tear said " the Black-Man
sleeps under a Nigga's shadow of **blood**."

Young, Black, & Handcuffed

To echo in the distance of far away places.
To be restless like the wind, and strong like the ox.
To be as free as a bird on a joyous spring day.
To be the sun that casts overpowering shadows
on the fortune of men.
To be the eagle that soars above storm clouds,
or the dove that brings calmness to the piercing
rays of the sun.
To be as cold and mystical like a panther looking
for pray.
To be in a death lock struggle with time.
Decisions come and cast a grim perspective
on freedom; and reality has revealed itself
in all of its' armor.
This is what it is to be **Young**.

From societies view:
Black is a color that is despised.
Black is evil and lurking, dark and menacing.
Black is to be put down, or kept in a realm of
unspeakable injustices.
To be slighted, looked over, made to feel
less than important,
less than real, and
less than human.
To be cursed by every ray of sunshine.
Looking like a hideous monster who
is misunderstood, and misguided in the
sea of hope.

Always languishing in the corner of a
closet door crying, hoping, and praying.
Always near the edge of prosperity, but
so close to the tempest of doom.
To be in a State of nothing, were
hardships do exist.
To always be in the valley of despair.
To wallow in the vast oceans of self-pity.
To always sit under the tree of injustices.
And then in the space of time, reality ran away,
and feelings of rage, jealousy, deceit, and envy
have come to comfort, and they are always there
on the twisted visage of the present day.
To be whipped in the unforgiving sun.
To be skinned and stripped of dignity.
To be lynched, hung, beaten, cursed,
spit upon and despised from every
corner of every city.
To be separated like laundry, tossed
in a pile and forgotten about.
To be left bleeding on cold-hard pavement.
Screaming in a distant time or place.
To have no clue, decision, or voice
in the seas of society, and
this is what it is to be **Black.**

Chains rattle with the air of discord,
or in the symphony of silence.
To be chained to a government
handout or program.
Always leaning on a crutch,
because there is no way

to stand alone and be counted.
To be in a hypnotic trance, of power
and fame, or to fall prey to the latest
evil plague called crack.
Responsibility is left at the door
like poor starving children.
To be tied up in the trite, materialistic
things in society; or pent-up in a cell
with the most hardened criminals.
The more the chain shakes the stronger it gets.
It has a hold on the hands, feet, and most importantly
the mind.
To forget about what is important and hold on to
things that only last a few seconds.
To have a feeling of power, energy and excitement,
but to always be handcuffed to them.
To feel powerful yet powerless.
To be in the confused realm of possibilities
and challenges that lie ahead.
Menial labor, hard hands, days of doom
and gloom, and no sunshine, no hope,
bound and gagged for failure without
an inkling of success.
This is what it is to be **handcuffed.**

Laughing in jest as time slips on by
like sand running through the fingers.
Languishing in a dark closet, searching
for respect in the sea of self-pity.
To have a voice that goes unheard
in the psyche of millions.

A handout is a crutch, which
provides something to stand on.
Ignorance is a chain that is endless
and never seems to die.
Failure is like a warm winter overcoat
that surrounds the very fabric of the being and soul.
Success is a distant shadow of a mountain that is
hard to climb and near impossible to reach form
the valley of despair. As the obstacles of life
grow bigger and bigger. While a shadow of blackness
may fade in a sunset , a somber song is sung.
This is what it is to be

Young, Black, & Handcuffed.

De La Coeur (from the heart)

To echo in the distance.
To be as free as a bird on a spring day;
or roam like a lion in the jungle.
To be as strong as an ox or restless like the wind.
Always looking for a new venue or challenge.
Searching for the dusk of ideas in the
ashbin of everyday life.
Crawling in the crawl-space of time looking
for a way out.
Strangled and cut-off by grim reports and statistics.

Languishing in the corner, begging for employment.
Searching for now and never looking beyond today.
It is about John, Jim, Larry, and Tyrone, struggling
to make an impression in a world that might seem faceless.
It is a mother crying, and wailing in the distant plains.
It is being handcuffed to the rainbow of flavors called drugs.

To be a government handout or a cause for
a special interest.
It is to have power and still be powerless.
To be led to the pool of insecurity only for someone
else's own personal gain.
To be lynched in the burning sun, or hung and beaten
by the injustices and broken promises of a country.
Locked in a jail cell, facing a cold ,dark and
painful existence.
To live like a pig in a hell-hole of no opportunity.
To be lynched by every corner of society.

Being called: Nigger, Coon, Spook, Jungle-Bunny,
Lazy, Shiftless, Inferior, A Dangerous M_ _ _ _ _ F_ _ _ _ _ _,
Stupid, Menacing, and Nasty.
Television is an escape from the harsh realities which
it also brings to light.
Life is never fair, but it is extremely tough when
faced with volatile situations.

Dancing of joy celebrating in accomplishments.
Knowing the roots or having the taken away.
Tomorrow is never promised and today may
never end.
But the true reality is that outside the white lines,
we languish in an eternal mistrust or in a funk of
darkness, that may never seem to end-
but in a pool of violence and terror against
one another.

Hatred

Hate- An intense hostility and aversion. **Antipathy.**

<u>Hatred</u>- Act of hating. Prejudiced hostility or animosity.

A Black Man Talks of Reaping

Heritage Bought and Sold

Southern Wilderness

Ghost Dances

Air of Supremacy

The Cross Burns

Women

Asleep at the Wheel

The Awakening

A Black Man Talks Of Reaping

A black man talks of reaping
under the hot oppressive sun.
A black man talks of reaping,
and never stops fighting till the
fight is done.

A black man talks of reaping
but watches as the blood of
generations lead to constant weeping.
A black man talks of reaping and yet
is constantly harassed, stereotyped and
put to the test.

A black man talks of reaping
in a society that teaches and
breeds hatred for one another
as well as everybody else.
A black man talks of reaping
with full intent. While the
system keeps sowing the
seeds of dismemberment.

This poem is based on the poem written by Langston Hughes

Heritage Bought & Sold

Heritage bought and sold,
all for wealth and all for gold.
For me, I'm treated less than human,
and less than real; while being locked
in a nightmarish world of inescapability.
Now, the only thing constant is the
screaming, writhing, throbbing pain
and agony felt throughout the body and soul.

When the still wind blows off the rough tides
of the sea, the ship starts to sway from side to side.
There are voices heard steering the ship this way and that,
but I do not hear them. I hear my family and my friends;
but they are only in a far distant land,
at a far distant place in time. And that
is the point of a deep well of sadness of
inexplicable bounds, that seem to have no end,
and a beginning which I can not find.

Chained to fear and doubt, are my hands.
Shackled to sorrow and shame are my feet.
And jangling in the air of discord is the sound
of those chains, shackles, and the crack of a whip.
On board this ship; as each new day arises, a
new struggle arises with it. Wayward wanders
being transported to a new place and time, whose
origin is unknown.
      But-
 For days on end and months gone by-

My dignity has been stripped,
My self-respect has slipped, and
my rage boils on the inside.
Now I make my home in the deep
abyss of a ship, which is my cage and
my din. I'm surrounded by thin
walls of rage and fury that turn
my spirit into dust. Dealing with-
another night of involuntary relieving of the body.
Another night of screaming women.
Another night of people praying to a God that
may or may not be. These are just more
dashed hopes, floating on the waters of oppression.
                    Now-
The ship continually bears the fury
of the uncontrollable sea. The
pain of the welts, and the death lock
chains still have not gone away ,and
are continually self-evident. But it
does not compare to the lashing, cutting,
and beating of poor souls. All for wealth
and all for gold, but the full flight of time
has not been foretold, about the legacy of
heritage bought and sold.

Southern Wilderness

Where the southern wind blows
the weeping willows shed their
tears of remorse for lost years.
The southern wilderness is dark,
haunting, and mysterious.
It is a place where the water
lays silent to protect its' secret
sins from being exposed.
It is a place where the trees
seem angry, and are lined-up
like an army prepared for an invasion.
Where the moss looks like a bunch of
tiny daggers ready to stab you to death.
The southern wilderness is now silent,
being accused of bodily theft.
The wilderness is where the grass
is greener than usual, because it
is fertilized with the fresh blood of today.
It is where the birds fly away,
because the wind howls in rage.
It is where the songs of hatred are sung,
and the moss is not the only thing that is hung.

The wilderness is where the black bodies hang,
because of the drunk prejudices of Billy Joe and the gang.
It is where the split personalities of time abound.
The sunshine brings hope, but the night is the
devils' playground.

It is where the torch of ignorance is passed down,
lighting the way for injustices to resound.
It is where peace and passion take two
different paths, splitting black bodies in half.
This is where the branch of perception
grows from the root of pride and prejudice.

Then under the slow rolling mist of cruel rain,
that branch of perception brings harsh terror and pain.
That branch took morals, and moral.
It took some samples, making
black people public examples.
It then took blood, turning
average men into thugs.
Most importantly, it took life
covering the wildernesses'
white lies in the darkness of night.
From that branch black bodies hang,
when the wind blows they all swang.
And then are buried in the water amidst
all the muck and the mud. The southern
wilderness is where the trees grow tall-
because they are all fertilized in blood.

The Ghost Dances

The ghost dances around a circle,
in the darkness of despair.
It dances when hearts are trampled.
It smiles when dreams are broken.
It laughs at the portrait of sadness that
hangs on the wall of misunderstanding.
>	The ghost still dances around the circle,
>	trying to break its infinite bond.
>	Trying to betray reality, and
>	curse the truth to make it a fallacy.
>	It attacks for no reason,-
>	It shackles the sober-minded
>	and makes it drunk with ignorance.

The ghost has no color, but-
uses that as the scapegoat of humanity.
It triumphed in past misconception,
It torments present acceptance, and-
It rejects the future's brightness, so
It can dim the light of prosperity.
>	The ghost still dances on what will be our graves.
>	It laughs in jest at our ignorance.
>	It smiles at our corrupt brutality.
>	It still lives in the deep psyche of prejudice,
>	which is governed by fear, just so
It can torment the circle of humanity.
The ghost still dances around the circle, just:

Releasing. **A.** **C**ancer. **I**nto. **S**ocieties'. **M**entality

"Air of Supremacy"

Stop! listen to the sound of nothing.
Look! and feel the air rise to its' supremacy.
Harken! But a gesture in a cause of trivial gains.

I stand alone against the rock of petulance.
I walk silently into the dungeon of fear.
I breathe the air of supremacy, only to be
lolled into a false sense of humanity.

I run on empty causes of distorted truths.
And this shall be my livelihood of fear.
I fret not for the impostors of what is true;
but for the truth not to be mixed with the
assorted facts of reality.

I have chosen my path, to guide the blinded soul
to a well of hope, that becomes others disparity.
I see the future dawn of present obstacles raking
against my mortality,
creating wounds of distrust and betrayal.

I seek truth only to find it is not in my world of reality,
but not lost on my cause. I feel the air of supremacy
rising to a different peak.
I still stand alone shrouded in darkness-
only left to deal with the delirium of my fear
and the ignorance of my stupidity.

The Cross Burns

During days of dust and fog, the heat of
oppression beat-down upon the oppressed.
It melted their hope,
It withered their faith,
It conquered their minds, and
prevented it from invading
open space.

In the background of darkness, somewhere
between stars and night, and quiet and mayhem
A Cross Burns -
In the Backyard
Off the interstate
On the road
Between the wild and the wilderness; and
In the reality of things lost and hoped for,
The Cross Burns -
hanging the oppressed,
crucifying the down-trodden, and
fanning the flames of degradation
against the dark skies of destruction.

The cross burns torturing the existence
of families. Lynching loved-ones,
leaving mothers crying, and shedding
their tears in the vast buckets of despair.
Leaving a distinct imprint on the psyche of generations
past, present, and future with the flames of degradation.

Leaving people crying in the shadows of hatred,
wailing for the hopes of loved ones lost and cared for.
Leaving a scar on the grass of equality, that is forever
burned in the minds of the fearful.

The cross burns, being doused with the kerosene
of stereotypes and lit with the match of fear.
It is the hopeful symbol of people covering
their white lies with the suffocating sheet
of ignorance and idolatry. It is the
pride and prejudice of individuals-
Who do not know,
Who do not care,
Who hide their lies of supremacy,
under the dark clouds of misunderstanding.

The cross burns holding freedom and opportunity
captive for those who can not see beyond its
bright glare. The cross is lit and struck with
violence, as the world turns on its ear.
Lynching the so-called distortion of
evil in the name of their only God-

FEAR.

Women

Out of the dust, man rose.
When his rib was taken, time froze.
And thus the saga of women began.
Life the interaction of woman and man.

She is the mother- Providing shelter for the future residents of earth
and eventually giving them life. She also gives closure in the underbelly of past memories, bringing present things to light.
She is the Nurturer- Providing tender love when necessary,
and affection in abundance. She can soothe pain with
her voice of reason and understanding.
She is the incarnation of love everlasting.
She loves when no one else can.
She loves when no one else will.
She provides support and caring
when things seem ill.
But-
She is considered an object, a trophy to be won
and shown off to everybody who wants to see.
She is considered an object of lust and vain fantasy.
She is considered an object who has no thought
being pimped, prostituted, and bought.
She has been raped of her love and tenderness.
She has been raped by certain members of the male-dominated society, and is now filled with bitterness.
She has been raped of her dreams and dignity,
paying the price for trying to gain liberty.
She has been beaten, for reasons
that change like the seasons.

She has been beaten to supposedly
restore order, but more chaos is created.
She has been beaten, heading toward
the road of total domination.
And through all of this, she has persevered and overcome.
She has become a strong force to be dealt with, because-
now she can think and stand alone. She no longer
Worships. Our. Masters. Every. Need.
Because she is no longer totally dependent.
Even though she has become the very symbol of
love, lust, and hatred.

    And-

In this very landscape she is still subjected to brutality.
The rib of man, still dealing with the harshness of reality.
And with all these atrocities tears are shed for hope
in the pool of equality. The Tears representing

Time. **E**mbraced. **A**nd. **R**emembered. **S**ymbolically

Asleep at the Wheel

Asleep at the wheel, somewhere between
having something and not having anything.
Asleep at the wheel, while traveling on the road
to destruction; which lies somewhere between
Red Tape and 1600 Penn. Avenue.

It seems we have fallen asleep, and we are
slumbering toward the dark spaces in the
infinite sky of possibilities. We are
asleep at the wheel, and seem to be
too blind to see reality.
To blind to see our own destruction.
To blind to see ourselves on the
twisted self-portrait of American politics.

We are everybody's favorite subject
Everybody's favorite game.
We are everybody's pawn, and
yet no one knows our name.
We are America's most hated,
loved, and used.
Yet from the mouths of diatribes
often abused.

We are asleep at the wheel snoring
into the white dissident plains.
Dreaming of hope for the future, while
riding in the presents' tormenting reality
and excruciating pain.

We are asleep at the wheel being
used as a crutch to better enable
the current politics to stand.
There are some liberals who
want to keep us in the slavery
of the government's pig sty.
They give some and take even more.
While the conservatives see us as
America's slimy sewer.

We are asleep at the wheel and the
road is coming to a dead end.
It is time to wake-up, but do
we know where to begin.
We are asleep at the wheel and
soon there will not be a we or an
us left. It is time to wake-up
because sleep is the cousin of
death.

Asleep at the wheel

Special Tribute   The Awakening

Sunday - September 15, 1963
The awakening of consciousness is at the
corner of chaos and mayhem .

The Indian Summer has set in and
the ever present heat of racial hatred
is hotter than the Alabama Summer is long.
Birmingham is about to be set ablaze in a
travesty of hatred, only leaving the charred
ruins of despair in the seas of equality .

The 5 o' clock shadow is growing misty now-
can you see it !
can you feel it !
can you touch it !
can you smell it!
can you taste the shadow of anticipation
that is about to paint a picture of horror,
on the landscape of injustice.
Now-
There are four little girls on their way to church
laughing, singing, and talking.
Not knowing they are taking their last steps .
Not knowing they are taking their last breaths .
Not knowing that they will be burned
by the searing flames of hatred.
Not knowing they will be cryogenically
frozen in innocence, while time took
a momentary rest in the bosom of insanity.

Then in a flash that was quicker than lightening
and louder than thunder, a bomb went off;
and four little girls were buried under
the rubble and debris of the 16th Street Church .

Now the tears of pain are confirming the loss
of innocence to the parents whose last trace
of their little girls lives is skeletal remains,
and the small bibles stuffed in their small
purses.

And the flash that shed four innocent lives
resonated throughout the country.
The flash left a deep scar on the complexion
of things to come.
That flash became the awakening, for the
rest of the country to take a look at the politics
of separate but equal,
Human and inhumane!
That flash made America look at its
two-sidedness in the mirror of a split society.

But-

Four little girls were sacrificed upon the altar
of humanity, showing how evil and corrupt
prejudice can be.
Four little girls were charred asunder,
Four little girls were swept away in
the flames of old Southern Justice.
Their burnt flesh became the awakening
of how strong the seed of hatred is when

it is planted in the fertile soil of misunderstanding. The awakening showed us who we were and became the catalyst for what we hope to be. That is a society melded together in love and equality not fear and persecution.
That is the way it was September 15, 1963
The Awakening.

War

A state or period of usually open and declared armed hostile conflict between states or nations.

A state of hostility, conflict, or antagonism. A struggle between opposing forces for an end.

The Manifesto

Cycle of Degradation

Bloody Sunday

War

Germ Warfare

Fields of Death

The Unknown Soldier

The Day the World Stopped

The Manifesto

Can you build a new world
on the face of the old one?
Can you build a new world
on the face of the old one?
As the earth revolves, the
old order of things seem to
be fading into a bleak existence.
Now its' shadows of greed and
materialism, are being absorbed
by the anger of the new order coalition.

The old order has dictatorships, to control
authority in vulgar displays of power.
Making the people live in hell's heat
of oppression.
With the propaganda
machines controlling thought there are
no transgressions.
Where people stand
on the firing line of ignorance, only to
be ravished by the bullets of hunger,
malnutrition, misinformation, despair,
and ridicule.
The old order has unwritten rules
that are words to live by, or die ignoring.
Like the majority rules, and the less
fortunate get exploited.
Like the ends justify the means,
but are the means leading to the end.

The old order rules with an iron fist of fear
 to keep up their oppression,
and to crush and annihilate any insurrection.

The old order judges harshly, by its
ideas of normalcy.
Divide and conquer is its' motto of diplomacy.
 Anyone living outside of the realm
is held in contempt of self-_expression,
and is viewed as committing multiple transgressions.

The old-order is:
slow to change,
stuck in its' ways,
revolves around tradition,
worships the ideals of hard-work,
prosperity, greed, sexism, classism,
racism, and self-ostracization,
self-degradation, self-exhortation,
and hiding its dark truths in the
closet and hoping they are never
brought to light.
 ~

The new order arises at the dawn
of chaos and anarchy. It has
absorbed the old orders' greed
and materialism; and molded it
into its blind rage and fury, that
breaks the rocks of compassion.

The new order is a global village,
where everyone has access to the
road of information. This is where
technology plays two roles one of
savior, and the other of permanent
destroyer.

**In the new order whatever
you are watching is actually watching you.**

Whatever you are hearing is listening to you.
Whatever you are feeling is actually feeling you. And
Whatever you are doing is actually killing you softly,
and hiding its harsh consequences for future generations
to discover.

The new order still has people living under
the thumb of oppression, but the propaganda
machines, are not controlling thought, just
making half-truths to keep people confused.
In the new order people do not stand on the
firing line of ignorance, but are being ravished
with fear by lethal injection.

The rules of this order are the same as the
old one. But the motto is different. The
motto of this new order is to fuck, kill, and prosper.
Meaning to fuck over anyone who will
let you, or is not hip to your scam.
Kill anyone that poses the biggest
opposition to your success.

And prosper by any means necessary.
In the New Order:
change is rampant,
tradition is crumbling
under the feet of reality.
Technology is one of the
many gods, it can create and destroy
with an instant touch. People worship
dead presidents, the ideals of easier is better,
greed is good, materialism, classism, racism,
ethnic diversity, multiculturalism, self- _expression,
depression, genocide, homicide, escapism,
self-ostracization, and nothing hides in darkness,
everything is bought to light.

So can you build a new world
on the face of the old one?
Possibly, because the more
things change the more they
stay the same. So as the new
world order progresses and cools;
The Earth still revolves around
the same old rules.
The Manifesto

Cycle of Degradation

The shadow of a mountain
is fading behind the sun.
Time and nature are at
conflict over the strife
and turmoil that has begun.

Man is at War again.
Man is destroying nature again.
Man is doing time a disservice again.

And in the backdrop of forgotten
yesterdays and endless tomorrow's
life is lived but time is borrowed.
Blood is shed for the lives taken.
Tears are shed for time wasted.
Humanity caught in the crossfire
of disagreement where no love
is tasted.

Are Heaven and Hell converging
on reality that is submerging
itself in an ocean of death?

And now the mountain of peace
is fading behind the sun of war;
just to get time and nature back
into harmony in this a Symphony of
Destruction.

"WAR"

Gloomy day sets in and I wonder
where I am. Death surrounds my
every move and it surrounds my
being. As the day grows my perception
grows bleary and I do not know why?

The sun tastes of blood, and I can feel
it clutching the dark corners of my soul.
The sky is caving in on me as the day
begins to die. I see my foes across the
long battlefield and they are trying to
kill me, because our countries share
different ideals in order to maintain peace.
The truth has been kept from me, and
I do not know why?

Reality has transformed
itself into a murderous being,
which I must accept even if it kills me.
This new reality I live in I want to dismiss,
as fiction in my imagination.

But the reality of this reality is that my sanity is
a fallacy of peaceful thought, trampled and buried
in the dust of time.

All of a sudden, I have been shot.
The cold bullet pierces my skin
and burns my flesh. Now I am

holding my heart and I do not
know why? Now I fall to the
dusty ground bleeding; and
my eyes grow heavier, my legs
grow weaker, and I am trying to
fight it and I do not know why?

I am crawling trying to climb out
of a pile of dead human flesh, and
I set my eyes on the little hole in the
sky, so I can wake-up from this
miserable dream, but I do not
know why? Truth has masked
itself and hidden from me in
an endless story of half-truths
known as the reality of this state
of mind called **WAR**.

Bloody Sunday

On this day the sky shines of an
orange glow that seems pessimistic.
Beyond the wind the boundless tree
 stretches forth onto an empty
landscape of nothing. It is this air
 that is caught in between natures'
 wall and window, and the dewdrops
of evil are always present
in this state of realism.

On that bloody battlefield
mothers' dream die, and new
men are made slaves to the
ignorance of stupidity and
the witchcraft of stubbornness.
The blood flows from these evil
veins, and the corrupt nature of it
is spreading among natures' relatives.

The air is thick with the firing of
bullets, bombs, and the moving of tanks.
It is these perilous things that lead us
closer to peaceful solutions to volatile
problems.

    War has made a century of wealthy people,
    and has created millenniums of impoverished ones.

War has made the quickening of the pulse and
the fervor of the spirit an obsolete reality that
is etched in an endless row of tombstones.

And this hell has grown bigger and the blood
drips and then dries in the memories of forever,
on the barren ground of yesterdays, and in the
fruitless thoughts of tomorrow. Now the
wind is still as nature weeps on times'
doorstep on a Sunday!
Bloody Sunday!

"Germ Warfare"

I was born in a lab,
I can turn open sores into scabs.
I am a germ.   Being used in
the name of science, and with
torture and torment I form a
deadly alliance.

In war I take many colors,
sizes, and shapes.
When you feel me,
your skin will start to bake.
When you feel me, you will
feel your body start to shake.
When you feel me roam in and
out of your flesh. I will sit back
and watch you rot to death.

You can not always see me, but you
know I am around.
You might see me in the
form of a big mushroom
acid cloud.
When you see me you see
the face of death in the eyes
of war.

When you see me you see me
in the form of a scab or a scar.

When you see me you , you
see the very essence of pain
and discomfort, no matter
where you are.

If you hear me, I give no
rhyme or reason. If you
hear me you hear the sound
of extreme coughing and
wheezing.
If you hear me you hear the
sound of sickness, that
denigrates the body with
sheer quickness.
If you hear me you hear the
moans, the screams, and the cries.
You hear me when the blood of death dries.

If you smell me, you
smell the rotting of flesh.
If you can smell me, you
smell the devil's breath.
If you can smell me,
you smell the stench;
of hundreds of dead bodies
buried in a ditch.

If you can taste me, I am
the taste of cruelty, in
the picnic of injustices.
I am the taste of deceit,
covering my flavor in

a sheet of lies and red-tape.
I am the taste of bitterness,
in the pool of hatreds' blood,
sweat, and tears.

I am a germ, causing
death and depression.
I am the conspiracy,
committing secret
transgressions.

I am a germ traveling
by air, destroying
people in the name
of science, called
Germ Warfare.

Fields of Death

The air is ripe with burnt flesh and blood.
The ground has become a mausoleum of bodies wrapped in mud.
The bullets are flying!
As it pierces the flesh a families dream is dying.

Time seems like it has come to an impasse.
Each day the sun rises peace is drowned in a blood bath.
The tanks roll like thunder from above.
But War is a cousin of Hatred's love.

The fields are ripe with the future that is dying.
The guns, the blood, and the bodies are multiplying.
Truth is held hostage because of the propaganda of
mass murder,
mass destruction,
mass annihilation,
mass abomination,
of culture and civilization.

The fields are ripe for this harvest season.
Which brings poverty, hunger, sickness, and diseases.
Which ravages the people's resolve and spirit.
There goes another bomb dropping, can you hear it!!!

Now there is a haze of fire and smoke.
Enough poison in the air to make the sky choke.
Now it is raining debris, rubble, and destruction.
There is no law and order; chaos is the only function.

The fields are where the last vestige of men are buried,
in screams,
in tears,
in blood,
in lies, and
in deception.
Waiting for the harvest of war,
to reap man's transgression.
        -Now
The air is still ripe with burnt flesh and blood.
The ground is still a mausoleum of bodies wrapped in mud.
Benevolent reality is taking its' last breath.
And is about to die on the bloody populated
fields of death!!.

The Unknown Soldier

The sun shines brightly,
and the wind blows crisply
through the rustling forest.
The sky is of the bluest hue
and its peace will reign on
this day.
The earth has been shaken
and the tomb of the unknown
soldier has been opened.

Footsteps are heard through the forest,
but who do they belong to?
These footsteps are now embedded in
the brains of every creature in the forest.
Now the wind has a new feel to it
and a different presence, but what is it?
A golden voice cries in the distilled
wilderness, and it falls softly into
a sea of tranquillity. But Oh! Where
is this ocean? Where does this mysterious
being lie?

Now the day is grim and gloomy
and it has no light to it. The sun
sets and the bloody uncertainty of
the future goes with it. The wind has
picked up force and is blowing down
everything in its path.   Swirling winds

and bone-chilling rain shake the earth
to its core, and these forces act upon
the consciousness of man, which
are shaped by the four corners of
the earth.

A battle weary person, who is unidentified, and
bloody bleeds hopeless uncertainty and despair.
The sky is gray and black and it breathes fire.
For it's happy that the golden voice has returned
home, and the majestic footprints are back to
their original origin; for the unknown soldier
has returned home to the bitter memories of
an unmarked grave.

The Day the World Stopped (An Essay)

I ate dinner at about 6:00 p.m. on January 15, 1991, and about that same time our country went into war. I did not really begin to understand the ramifications of this war, until I got to school the next day.

The next day at school, I was talking to my friends and they all kept saying and harping on the fact that we kicked some Iraqi ass. We kicked their asses! And for what reasons, for what thought. I do not think it dawned on any of us what the hell was going on, until the principal Mr. Heiser come on the intercom and said "let's have a moment of silence for our troops."

The next minute seemed as a thousand years in the sands of time. Complete and eerie silence fell over the class. It seemed that everybody had an emotionless blank stare of confusion on their faces, as if somebody held a gun to their heads. When in actuality the class was looking right at a cold bullet of reality that had been fired at sudden impact. They looked puzzled as if to say "what did we do, what is going on, can we really be at war, and why?" The look on Mike's face told a story that ran the gamut of emotions of rage, anger, fear, anxiety, and confusion. The look on his face was saying "what have I done wrong, and why in the hell is this happening now?"

And for one minute the earth stood still, while rendering her inhabitants helpless, restlessly captive of something they could imagine but not feel the full ramifications of unless they have been through it.

They say time heals all wounds, even the wounds of war. Time is now raging with anger and fury to clean up the mess he hath wroth upon us. This is just a microcosm of our emotions wrapped up in one min-

ute. For now we look into the sand's of the hour glass and see our emotions spilled on the floor they are: confusion, anxiety for loved ones, fear, disarray, disgust, and anger. For this was just one minute in the complex journey of our emotions traveling through the facade of the soul.
And that's the way it was on January 16, 1991.

Reflection

Millennium

A new millennium is on the cusp.
Time incarnated rising like the sun.
A new millennium fills the air of
despair with the aroma of hope.
A new millennium comes as a comfort
to those who can not cope.
Reality like lightning strikes with
a forceful presence now, but will
it strike when a new millennium
comes in a thunderous uproar?

-So
 Will our winters be of the nuclear variety?
Will hope spring eternal, while the flames
of degradation continue to heat-up and
engulf humanity in its rage?
Will summers' heat continue to let
fear perspirate our brains?
Will the leaves of tradition continue to
fall on the grass of change?

A new millennium is starting to form and
take shape in the shadows of chaos and turmoil.

-So
Will life's questions be answered, or
will life's answers be questioned?
Will the bridge of ignorance crumble
in the ocean of knowledge?

Will humanity become one race,
instead of racing to keep pace with
perception?
Will the truth become whole again,
and not cut-up and handed out by the
slice?
Will humanity end?
Will good and evil finally settle their war?
Will the Saints ever win the Super Bowl?
A new millennium is dawning, and the
erstwhile dimensions of now are fading
into the abyss of memories which may
or may not be found again.
-So
 Will life ever be pure?
Will we ever find a cure for:
AIDS, STD's, Alzheimer's, Cancer,
or any other deadly diseases that may
pop-up.
Will war continue to be the fastest
way to reduce the population, and
create poverty, homelessness, and pollution?
Will there be a new world order?
      A new millennium is rising.
      A new age is dawning.
      A new day is calling.
      A new year is coming in
more than 1,000 ways.
A new century is on the
next block; once we turn off
the old one, once we turn off
the old one.

Thanks, and Dedications:

First and foremost, I want to thank God for blessing me with the talent to write and to express myself in a literary manner. I also want to thank my family for being the stabilizing force in my life, and providing support to allow me to grow into the person that I am. I also want to thank Thompson Temple C.O.G.I.C for providing opportunities to be heard.

X-tra special thanks go out to the following people:

Julie Savory - for listening when nobody else did.

James Potter - for being there, and being a good soundboard

Colan Niles - for providing a different persepctive on things.

David Thompson Jr. - for being a very good friend

Cleveland Lawrence - for being an example of overcoming the odds and achieving your dreams

About the Author

Brian Swanson was born in Tuscaloosa, Alabama and grew up in New Orleans, Louisiana. He is currently a Manufacturing Equipment Tech working a billion dollar tech cpmapany in the Pacific Northwest.

Outside of this book of prose he has written many short-stories and poems yet to be published.

Please be on the lookout for his next book of prose/poetry:

What's wrong with the world;

the death, burial, and resurrection.

And many Short stories ready to amaze the masses.

www.ingramcontent.com/pod-product-compliance
Lightning Source LLC
Chambersburg PA
CBHW030159100526
44592CB00009B/352